ENGINEERING FOR DISASTER

# ENGINEERING FOR SPACE DISASTERS

by Marne Ventura

FOCUS READERS.
NAVIGATOR

# WWW.FOCUSREADERS.COM

Copyright © 2021 by Focus Readers®, Lake Elmo, MN 55042. All rights reserved. No part of this book may be reproduced or utilized in any form or by any means without written permission from the publisher.

Focus Readers is distributed by North Star Editions:
sales@northstareditions.com | 888-417-0195

Produced for Focus Readers by Red Line Editorial.

Content Consultant: Ray Sedwick, Professor of Aerospace Engineering, University of Maryland

Photographs ©: JSC/NASA, cover, 1, 7, 11; KSC/NASA, 4–5, 8–9, 21, 25; MSFC/NASA, 13, 14–15; Shutterstock Images, 17; AFRC/NASA, 18–19; Red Line Editorial, 23; Joel Kowsky/HQ/NASA, 26–27; Kim Shiflett/KSC/NASA, 29

**Library of Congress Cataloging-in-Publication Data**
Names: Ventura, Marne, author.
Title: Engineering for space disasters / Marne Ventura.
Description: Lake Elmo, MN : Focus Readers, 2021. | Series: Engineering for disaster | Includes index. | Audience: Grades 4-6
Identifiers: LCCN 2019057409 (print) | LCCN 2019057410 (ebook) | ISBN 9781644933817 (hardcover) | ISBN 9781644934579 (paperback) | ISBN 9781644936092 (ebook pdf) | ISBN 9781644935330 (hosted ebook)
Subjects: LCSH: Space vehicle accidents--History--Juvenile literature. | Astronautics--Accidents--History--Juvenile literature. | Aeronautics--Safety measures--Juvenile literature.
Classification: LCC TL867 .V46 2021  (print) | LCC TL867  (ebook) | DDC 629.47--dc23
LC record available at https://lccn.loc.gov/2019057409
LC ebook record available at https://lccn.loc.gov/2019057410

Printed in the United States of America
Mankato, MN
082020

# ABOUT THE AUTHOR

Marne Ventura has written more than 100 children's books. She writes about science, technology, engineering and math, arts and crafts, and the lives of creative people. A former teacher, she holds a degree from the University of California. Marne and her husband live on the central coast of California.

# TABLE OF CONTENTS

### CHAPTER 1
## Columbia  5

### CHAPTER 2
## Takeoff Challenges  9

### CHAPTER 3
## Flight Challenges  15

### CHAPTER 4
## Landing Challenges  19

# CASE STUDY
## Ascent Abort-2  24

### CHAPTER 5
## Future Challenges  27

Focus on Engineering for Space Disasters • 30
Glossary • 31
To Learn More • 32
Index • 32

## CHAPTER 1

# COLUMBIA

Disaster struck on the morning of February 1, 2003. The space shuttle *Columbia* was returning to Earth. It had spent 15 days in space. The shuttle would cross over Texas. Then it would land at Kennedy Space Center (KSC) in Florida.

Engineers at KSC approved the shuttle for **reentry** into Earth's atmosphere.

*Columbia* **first reached space in 1981. It went on 28 missions in total.**

They tracked the shuttle's tire pressure and the wings' heat. Nine minutes later, the engineers lost readings from the left wing. They called the shuttle crew. But they got no answer. The shuttle wasn't showing up on **radar**. Meanwhile, people in Texas saw **debris** falling from the sky.

*Columbia* had broken apart during reentry. The disaster destroyed the shuttle. All seven astronauts died. Later, engineers found the cause. A chunk of foam had broken off from the fuel tank during liftoff. It hit the shuttle's left wing and made a hole. Hot air entered the wing during reentry. It caused the shuttle to quickly fall apart.

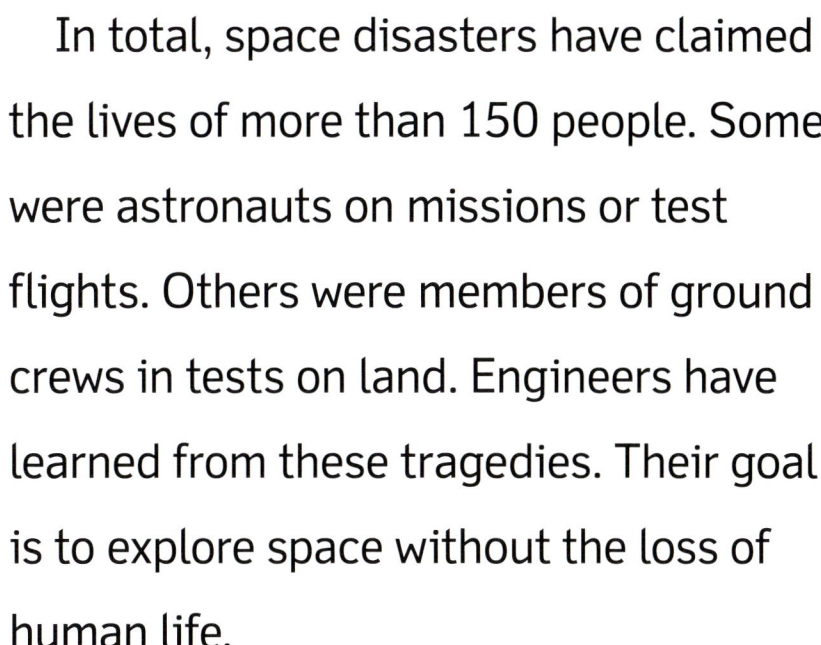

More than 500 people have traveled to space.

In total, space disasters have claimed the lives of more than 150 people. Some were astronauts on missions or test flights. Others were members of ground crews in tests on land. Engineers have learned from these tragedies. Their goal is to explore space without the loss of human life.

## CHAPTER 2
# TAKEOFF CHALLENGES

Takeoff presents many challenges for engineers. Launching a spacecraft requires a huge burst of energy. Rockets burn fuel to give the spacecraft power. They help the spacecraft travel more than 25,000 miles per hour (40,000 km/h). A spacecraft that does not go fast enough will not be able to achieve Earth **orbit**.

**Takeoffs produce large amounts of smoke and fire.**

9

It will crash back to Earth. Also, fuel gets very hot when burned. It gives off hot gases. It expands. The danger of fire and explosion is high.

In 1986, the *Challenger* shuttle blew up 73 seconds after liftoff. All seven

## ROUND-TRIP MISSIONS

Rockets must reach very high speeds to escape a planet's **gravity**. So, they need to burn a lot of fuel. This fact makes missions to other planets a challenge. A spacecraft needs fuel to leave Earth. It also needs fuel to take off again from the other planet. Fuel adds weight to the spacecraft. The heavier the spacecraft, the more fuel is needed for liftoff. Engineers are developing better fuels and lighter materials to solve this problem.

*Challenger* takes off from a launch pad at KSC in 1986.

crewmembers died. A frozen O-ring caused the disaster. This ring covered a joint in one of the rockets. It was supposed to keep hot gases from leaking out. But the ring failed. The rocket burned fuel at liftoff. Hot gases leaked out.

The leak threw the shuttle off course. And the force of the leak broke the shuttle apart. Debris from the shuttle fell into the Atlantic Ocean.

After the disaster, NASA improved its safety program. It created a new team to check and recheck the spacecraft. Engineers improved the sealing system. They used backup O-rings. They better **insulated** the joints.

Rockets burn fuel to launch spacecraft. But the fuel weighs a lot. In 2017, NASA tested an X3 ion **thruster**. The design uses a stream of ions. Ions are atoms with an electric charge. They flow out the back of the thruster. This action pushes

Engineers insert O-rings into the Ares crew launch vehicle in 2008.

the thruster forward. The X3 can go much faster than rockets in space. It also adds much less weight to a spacecraft than rockets do. The X3 will help future spacecraft move through space.

CHAPTER 3

# FLIGHT CHALLENGES

The International Space Station (ISS) orbits 250 miles (400 km) above Earth. Astronauts use the station. They study how living in space affects people.

Spending months in space puts people at risk of cancer. Spacecraft are often made of aluminum. This metal does not protect people from space radiation.

**The first section of the ISS launched in 1998. Astronauts have added to the ISS since then.**

So, engineers are testing plastic suits and spacecraft. Plastic is light and strong. It can help protect humans from radiation.

In **microgravity**, human bodies don't get the workout they would get on Earth. As a result, muscles and bones lose strength and mass. Engineers are testing artificial-gravity devices. One device is a

## SPACE GARDENING

Running out of food during a long spaceflight would be a disaster. So, ISS astronauts are studying how to grow food in space. On Earth, plants take in water through their roots. In microgravity, water doesn't trickle down to the roots. Engineers designed tubes that force water downward. ISS astronauts have successfully grown lettuce using these tubes.

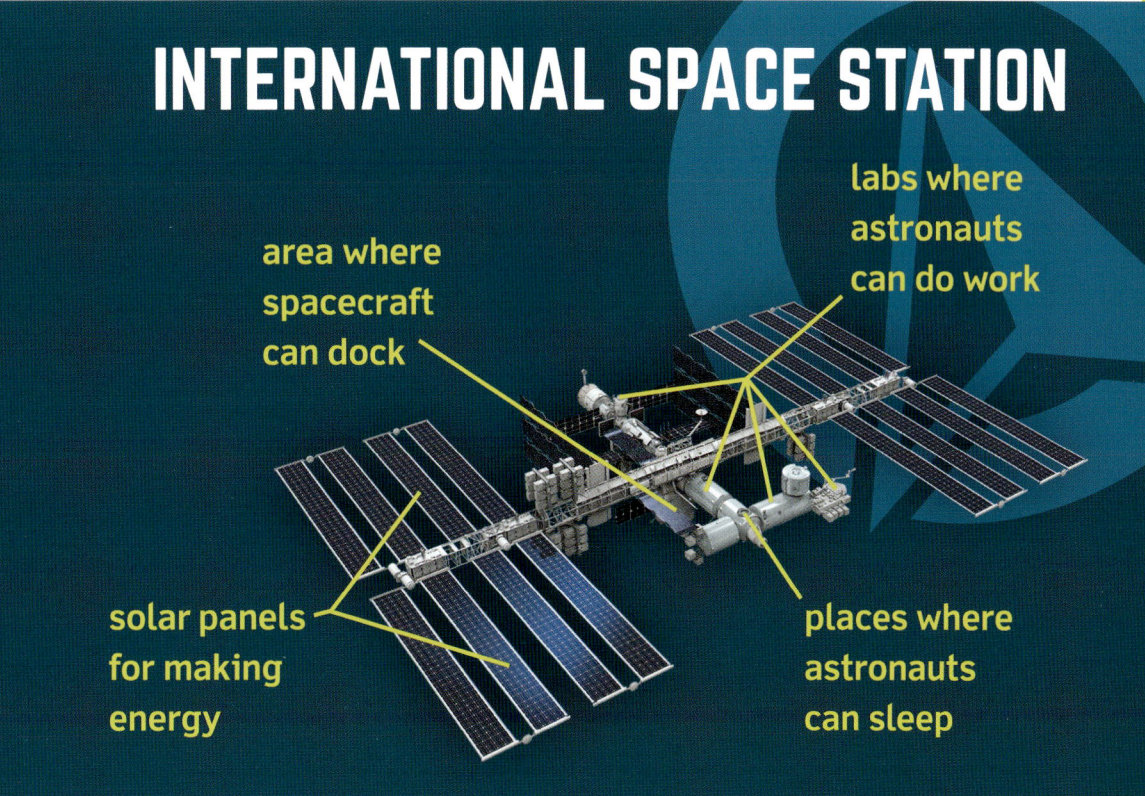

# INTERNATIONAL SPACE STATION

- labs where astronauts can do work
- area where spacecraft can dock
- solar panels for making energy
- places where astronauts can sleep

spinning platform. People lie on a board. They pedal a wheel to make the device spin around. This spin creates a force similar to gravity. Engineers designed this device to help astronauts stay healthy in space.

17

CHAPTER 4

# LANDING CHALLENGES

Landing a spacecraft is tricky. Earth's gravity pulls the spacecraft in. The spacecraft must slow down enough to avoid crashing. A spacecraft returning from the ISS travels 17,500 miles per hour (28,000 km/h). To slow it down, thrusters rotate the spacecraft. The spacecraft gets into a tail-first position.

**Workers prepare to bring a shuttle back to KSC after a safe landing in California.**

Then it fires its engines against the direction of motion. The spacecraft slows down. By now, it has reached Earth's atmosphere. Gravity pulls it in. The spacecraft is still moving very fast. Its temperature rises to thousands of degrees. High heat and speed make landing very dangerous.

*Columbia* was traveling 12,500 miles per hour (20,100 km/h) when it broke apart. The hole in its wing could not take the heat and pressure of reentry. After the disaster, NASA engineers redesigned the shuttle's tank. Astronauts began using cameras and a robotic arm. They checked for damage during liftoff. Also, engineers

A parachute slows the shuttle *Discovery* as it lands on a runway at KSC.

made plans to use the ISS as a safety stop. Astronauts could stop there if they found damage.

After the *Columbia* disaster, engineers started working on a new type of spacecraft. They designed Orion. It first launched in 2014. It has seats that closely fit the astronauts' bodies. Engineers used race car seats as a model.

The new seats support and cushion the body during a crash. Engineers also designed better-fitting seat belts. They modeled them after children's car seats. The new belts adjust to fit all body sizes.

## PARACHUTES

Vladimir Komarov was a Russian astronaut. He was the first human to die in a space disaster. In 1967, Soviet spacecraft Soyuz 1 reentered Earth's atmosphere. But the parachutes designed for landing failed. The spacecraft crashed to the ground. Engineers have designed a new parachute system for Orion. Earth's atmosphere will slow the spacecraft from 20,000 to 325 miles per hour (32,000 to 520 km/h). Then the parachutes will slow the spacecraft to 20 miles per hour (32 km/h).

Engineers redesigned spacesuits, too. In an emergency, a spacecraft's air pressure might drop. That would lead to a loss of oxygen. Astronauts need oxygen to breathe. If air pressure drops, the new suits will inflate on their own. They will protect astronauts from a loss of oxygen.

## BETTER SPACESUITS

### LIFE SUPPORT
The suit gives oxygen, takes away carbon dioxide, and includes a radio for communications.

### UV PROTECTION
The helmet's visor has a thin coating of gold, which protects the astronaut from the sun's harmful rays.

### JETPACK
An emergency jetpack allows the astronaut to move around during spacewalks.

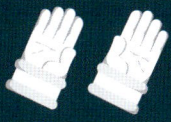
### GLOVES
The glove's fingers are flexible, but air pressure makes them hard to bend.

### SAFETY TETHER
A long tether connects the astronaut to the spacecraft.

### TEMPERATURE CONTROL
The suit protects the astronaut from the big changes in temperature in space.

## CASE STUDY

# ASCENT ABORT-2

Engineers knew the O-ring on *Challenger* might be a problem. They also knew the wing of *Columbia* had been damaged. But the shuttles had already launched. Engineers didn't have a way to stop the missions.

In 2019, NASA tested its new Launch Abort System. To abort is to stop something earlier than was planned. Engineers designed the system to return astronauts to safety during a launch. They called the test Ascent Abort-2.

Engineers attached the system to an Orion test spacecraft. The spacecraft shot up 6 miles (10 km) over Florida. The system was designed to abort if there were signs of trouble. During the test, the system received a signal of trouble. In response, the system went to work. A rocket motor pulled the crew module away from the rocket.

The Launch Abort System and a test version of Orion launch during a test in 2019.

The motor turned the module in the right direction. The module safely splashed down in the Atlantic Ocean. The Launch Abort System worked. With this technology, astronauts can stay safe even if something goes wrong during liftoff.

25

CHAPTER 5

# FUTURE CHALLENGES

In the late 2010s, NASA scheduled the Artemis missions to the moon. The missions would use the Orion spacecraft. Engineers had designed it for safety. They planned to launch Orion from KSC in Florida. First, Orion would launch in a test flight without astronauts inside. Then, astronauts would fly in Orion.

**A spacesuit engineer wears the suit that astronauts would wear on the Artemis mission.**

The missions' goal was to land American astronauts on the moon by 2024. NASA planned to later send astronauts to the planet Mars.

NASA planned to use the moon as a base for astronauts. The moon is approximately 1,000 times farther from Earth than the ISS. Mars is 34 million miles (55 million km) away from Earth. Engineers planned to test ways to travel such large distances. They hoped to learn how to make fuel and oxygen from materials on the moon's surface. Then astronauts could use the moon as a supply base. They wouldn't have to carry as much weight on their spacecraft.

Engineers add a heat shield to the Orion crew module in 2018.

Space travel is a dangerous challenge. Scientists and astronauts search for answers about the universe. Engineers search for ways to keep astronauts safe.

# FOCUS ON
# ENGINEERING FOR SPACE DISASTERS

*Write your answers on a separate piece of paper.*

1. Write a letter to a friend describing the challenges of liftoff.

2. If given the opportunity, would you want to visit the ISS? Why or why not?

3. When did the damage that caused the *Columbia* disaster occur?
    - **A.** during liftoff
    - **B.** during orbit
    - **C.** during reentry

4. Why is it important for astronauts to maintain muscle strength and bone mass in space?
    - **A.** so that they can survive the intense heat and gas pressure of reentry
    - **B.** so that when they return to Earth, they are strong enough to withstand Earth's gravity
    - **C.** so that they are strong enough to survive the effects of space radiation

*Answer key on page 32.*

# GLOSSARY

**debris**
The remains of something broken.

**gravity**
The force one object has on another due to the mass of each object and how far apart they are.

**insulated**
Stopped heat from getting in or out.

**microgravity**
When the downward pull of gravity is very small compared with the forward motion of an object such as a space station.

**orbit**
The curved path of a spacecraft or space object around a planet, moon, or star.

**radar**
An instrument that locates things by bouncing radio waves off them.

**reentry**
Coming back into Earth's atmosphere after space travel.

**thruster**
An engine that changes a spacecraft's flight path.

# TO LEARN MORE

## BOOKS

Hamilton, John. *International Space Station: The Science Lab in Space*. Minneapolis: Abdo Publishing, 2018.

Kruesi, Liz. *Discover Space Exploration*. Minneapolis: Lerner Publications, 2017.

Raum, Elizabeth. *Fighting to Survive Space Disasters: Terrifying True Stories*. North Mankato, MN: Capstone Publishing, 2020.

## NOTE TO EDUCATORS

Visit **www.focusreaders.com** to find lesson plans, activities, links, and other resources related to this title.

# INDEX

Artemis missions, 27–28
Ascent Abort-2, 24
atmosphere, 5, 20, 22

*Challenger*, 10–11, 24
*Columbia*, 5–6, 20–21, 24

fuel, 6, 9–12, 28

gravity, 10, 16–17, 19–20

International Space Station (ISS), 15–17, 19, 21, 28

Kennedy Space Center (KSC), 5, 27
Komarov, Vladimir, 22

landing, 19–20, 22
Launch Abort System, 24–25
liftoff, 6, 10–11, 20, 25

Mars, 28
microgravity, 16

orbit, 9, 15
O-ring, 11–12, 24
Orion, 21–22, 24, 27

parachutes, 22

radiation, 15–16
reentry, 5–6, 20, 22

Soyuz 1, 22
spacesuits, 23

X3 ion thruster, 12–13

Answer Key: **1.** Answers will vary; **2.** Answers will vary; **3.** A; **4.** B